Usborne
Sticker Atlas
of Britain and
Northern Ireland

Stephanie Turnbull

Designed by Doriana Berkovic and Sam Chandler

Illustrated by Colin King

Additional illustrations by
Stuart Trotter and Non Figg

Britain and the UK

Britain is the largest island in Europe. It is made up of three countries: England, Scotland and Wales. Britain and Northern Ireland are together known as the United Kingdom (UK). The rest of Ireland and the Isle of Man are not part of the UK.

Internet links
For links to websites where you can find out lots of amazing facts about Britain and Northern Ireland, go to
www.usborne-quicklinks.com

Shetland Islands

Western Isles

Orkney Islands

NORTH SEA

SCOTLAND

ATLANTIC OCEAN

EDINBURGH

NORTHERN IRELAND
BELFAST

Isle of Man

REPUBLIC OF IRELAND

IRISH SEA

ENGLAND

WALES

This map shows Britain, Northern Ireland and other small islands that are part of the United Kingdom. Each country's capital is marked.

CARDIFF

LONDON

Isles of Scilly

ENGLISH CHANNEL

UK flags

The flags of England, Scotland and Ireland combine to form the flag of the UK. This is called the Union Flag, but is usually known as the Union Jack. Wales had already united with England when the first Union Jack was created, in 1606, so the Welsh flag isn't included in the design. The St. Patrick's Cross was included when Ireland became part of the United Kingdom in 1801, and still represents Northern Ireland.

The Union Flag

St. George's Cross of England

The Red Dragon of Wales

St. Andrew's Cross of Scotland

St. Patrick's Cross of Ireland

People and language

There are over 60 million people living in the UK. The main language is English, although Scotland, Wales and Ireland have their own languages too. Many people from other parts of the world have also settled in Britain.

Governments

The UK is run by an elected government, led by the Prime Minister, and the Queen is the head of state. Wales, Northern Ireland and Scotland also have their own governments, which help to run each country.

This is the Saint Edward's Crown, which is worn at the coronation of new kings and queens.

Locator maps

The maps on pages 4–29 each have a small locator map of the UK next to them. The red part tells you which area is shown on the large map.

This locator map goes with the large map of East Anglia.

How to use this book

The stickers in this book show some of the UK's most famous sights and events, including castles, museums, theme parks, sports and festivals. To find out where the stickers go, match them to the black and white outlines on the maps. You can check what the stickers show by finding their matching numbers on the lists next to the maps. There's also a full list of stickers and their page numbers at the back of the book to help you.

London

London is the capital city of England. Around seven million people live there, making it Europe's largest city. It has all kinds of museums and galleries, as well as many large parks. This map shows the middle of the city, where many museums and shops are found.

Internet links

For links to websites where you can find out more about London, go to www.usborne-quicklinks.com

Dinosaur display

The Natural History Museum is one of the largest museums in Europe. It is famous for its spectacular dinosaur exhibits, which include lifelike moving models and a 26m (85ft) long Diplodocus skeleton.

Chinatown

Chinatown is a small part of central London that has become one of the capital's main tourist attractions. Its streets are lined with Chinese restaurants, and every year local Chinese people have a big parade to celebrate Chinese New Year.

London stickers

1 Tower of London
2 Shakespeare's Globe
3 British Museum
4 Clock tower, Houses of Parliament
5 Guard, Buckingham Palace
6 London Eye
7 Hamleys toy store
8 St. Paul's Cathedral
9 Nelson's Column
10 Dinosaur, Natural History Museum
11 Tower Bridge
12 Parrot, London Zoo
13 HMS Belfast
14 Boating, Hyde Park
15 London bus
16 Chinese New Year parade

Big wheel

One of the best ways to see London is from the London Eye, an enormous wheel on the south bank of the Thames. Up to 15,000 passengers a day ride in its enclosed capsules.

The West Country

The southwestern corner of England is known as the West Country. It has sandy beaches along the coast, and lush fields and high moors further inland. The West Country is often warmer and sunnier than the rest of Britain.

Rocky ruins

Tintagel Castle stands high on a cliff top beside the Atlantic Ocean. The castle was built in the thirteenth century and is now in ruins. Many people believe that King Arthur, a legendary British ruler in ancient times, was born in an older castle on the same spot.

Giant domes

The Eden Project, in Cornwall, consists of two sets of linked domes that form two huge greenhouses. Different climates from around the world are recreated inside the greenhouses, so that thousands of amazing plants are able to grow there.

Lundy Island

Barnstaple c
Bideford Ba

Hartland Point

ATLANTIC OCEAN

Bude

Bodmin Mo

Newquay

St. Austell

Whitsand Bay

Redruth

Truro

Falmouth

Penzance

Land's End

Mount's Bay

Isles of Scilly

Lizard Point

Internet links
For links to websites where you can find out more about this region, go to
www.usborne-quicklinks.com

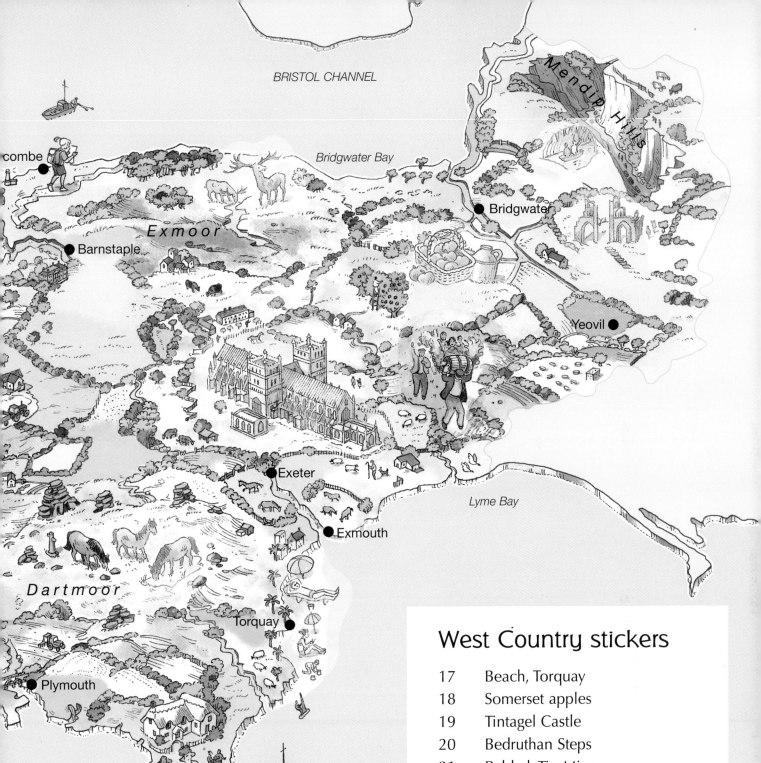

BRISTOL CHANNEL

Mendip Hills

Bridgwater Bay

Bridgwater

combe

Exmoor

Barnstaple

Yeovil

Exeter

Lyme Bay

Exmouth

Dartmoor

Torquay

Plymouth

Start Point

Fiery festival

The town of Ottery St. Mary holds an unusual festival on November 5th each year. Local men run through the streets, carrying barrels of burning tar. When the barrels are too hot to hold, they are rolled along the ground until they fall apart.

West Country stickers

17 Beach, Torquay
18 Somerset apples
19 Tintagel Castle
20 Bedruthan Steps
21 Poldark Tin Mine
22 Tropical garden, Tresco
23 Deer, Exmoor National Park
24 Exeter Cathedral
25 St. Michael's Mount
26 Ponies, Dartmoor
27 Surfing, Atlantic Ocean
28 Wookey Hole Caves
29 Ottery St. Mary fire festival
30 Eden Project
31 Glastonbury Abbey

The South Coast

Along England's south coast are many wide beaches, steep white cliffs and popular seaside resorts. Most visitors to Britain arrive at London's airports, the south coast's busy sea ports, or come via the Channel Tunnel rail link.

Yacht races

Every August, hundreds of yachts from all over the world take part in boat races in the sea around the Isle of Wight. The eight-day event is known as Cowes Week.

Andover

Basingstoke

Hampshire Downs

Winchester

Cranborne Chase

New Forest

Southampton

North Dorset Downs

Portsmouth

Selsey Bill

Bournemouth

Poole

The Solent

Lyme Bay

South Dorset Downs

Newport

Chesil Beach

Weymouth

Isle of Portland

The Needles

Isle of Wight

Bill of Portland

St. Catherine's Point

Cricket champions

In the 1750s, one of England's most famous cricket clubs was formed in the village of Hambledon. The team became very successful and they recorded many of the rules that are still used. The game of cricket might have started as far back as the 1200s.

City by the sea

Brighton is a lively seaside town. It has a long pier, crammed with amusement arcades and souvenir stalls. Another famous landmark is the Royal Pavilion, a huge white building that is designed to look like an Indian palace.

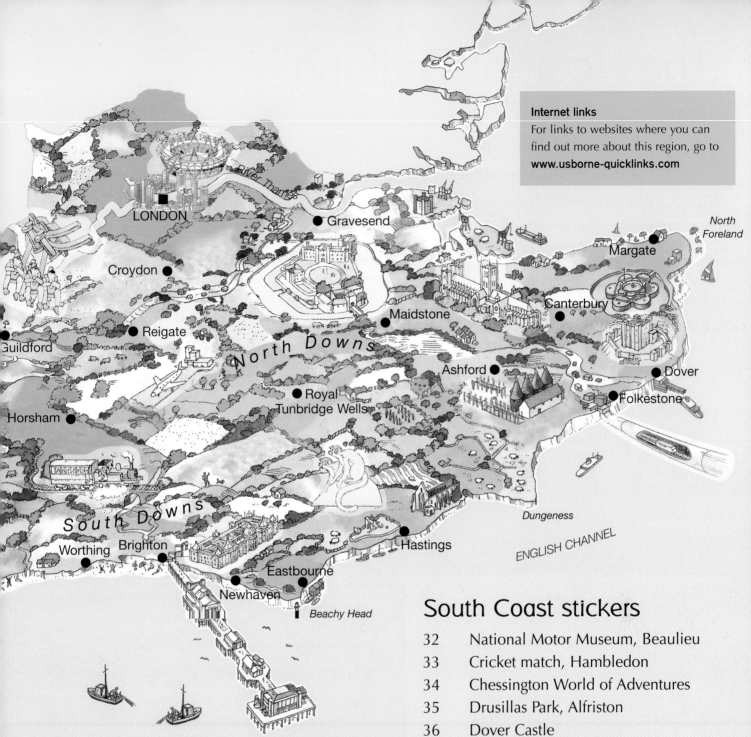

LONDON

Gravesend

Croydon

Margate

North Foreland

Canterbury

Maidstone

Reigate

N o r t h   D o w n s

Guildford

Ashford

Dover

Royal Tunbridge Wells

Folkestone

Horsham

S o u t h   D o w n s

Worthing   Brighton

Hastings

Dungeness

Eastbourne

ENGLISH CHANNEL

Newhaven

Beachy Head

Underwater trains

The Channel Tunnel is the world's longest undersea rail link. It lies under the English Channel and connects Britain and France. Fast passenger trains take just 21 minutes to travel from one end to the other.

South Coast stickers

32	National Motor Museum, Beaulieu
33	Cricket match, Hambledon
34	Chessington World of Adventures
35	Drusillas Park, Alfriston
36	Dover Castle
37	HMS Victory, Portsmouth
38	Royal Pavilion, Brighton
39	Channel Tunnel
40	Maiden Castle hill fort, Dorchester
41	Gatwick Airport
42	Canterbury Cathedral
43	Yachting, near the Isle of Wight
44	Leeds Castle
45	Bluebell Railway, near East Grinstead
46	Farnborough International air show
47	Olympic Stadium, London

The Heart of England

The central part of England contains historic houses and mysterious ancient sites. There is also beautiful countryside, such as the Chilterns, with their rolling chalk hills, and the Cotswolds, which are dotted with pretty villages.

Amazing maze

Longleat House, in Wiltshire, is an Elizabethan mansion that is open to the public. The gardens around it contain a safari park and a massive hedge maze, made up of more than 16,000 yew trees.

Cheltenham

Gloucester

Forest of Dean

River Severn

Cotswold Hills

Stroud

Cirencester

River Thames

Vale of the White Horse

Swindon

Marlborough Downs

Chippenham

Bristol

Bristol Channel

Bath

River Avon

Kennet-Avon Canal

Salisbury Plain

Salisbury

Internet links
For links to websites where you can find out more about this region, go to
www.usborne-quicklinks.com

Map labels (reading across the illustrated map):

Banbury

River Great Ouse

Bedford

Milton Keynes

Stevenage

Luton

Bishop's Stortford

Aylesbury

St. Albans

Oxford

Abingdon

rkshire Downs

Chiltern Hills

High Wycombe

River Thames

Reading

River Kennet

Slough

Chalk horse

The White Horse is a huge figure that was cut into a chalky hillside thousands of years ago. Some people believe that it shows an ancient horse god, while others think it may be a dragon.

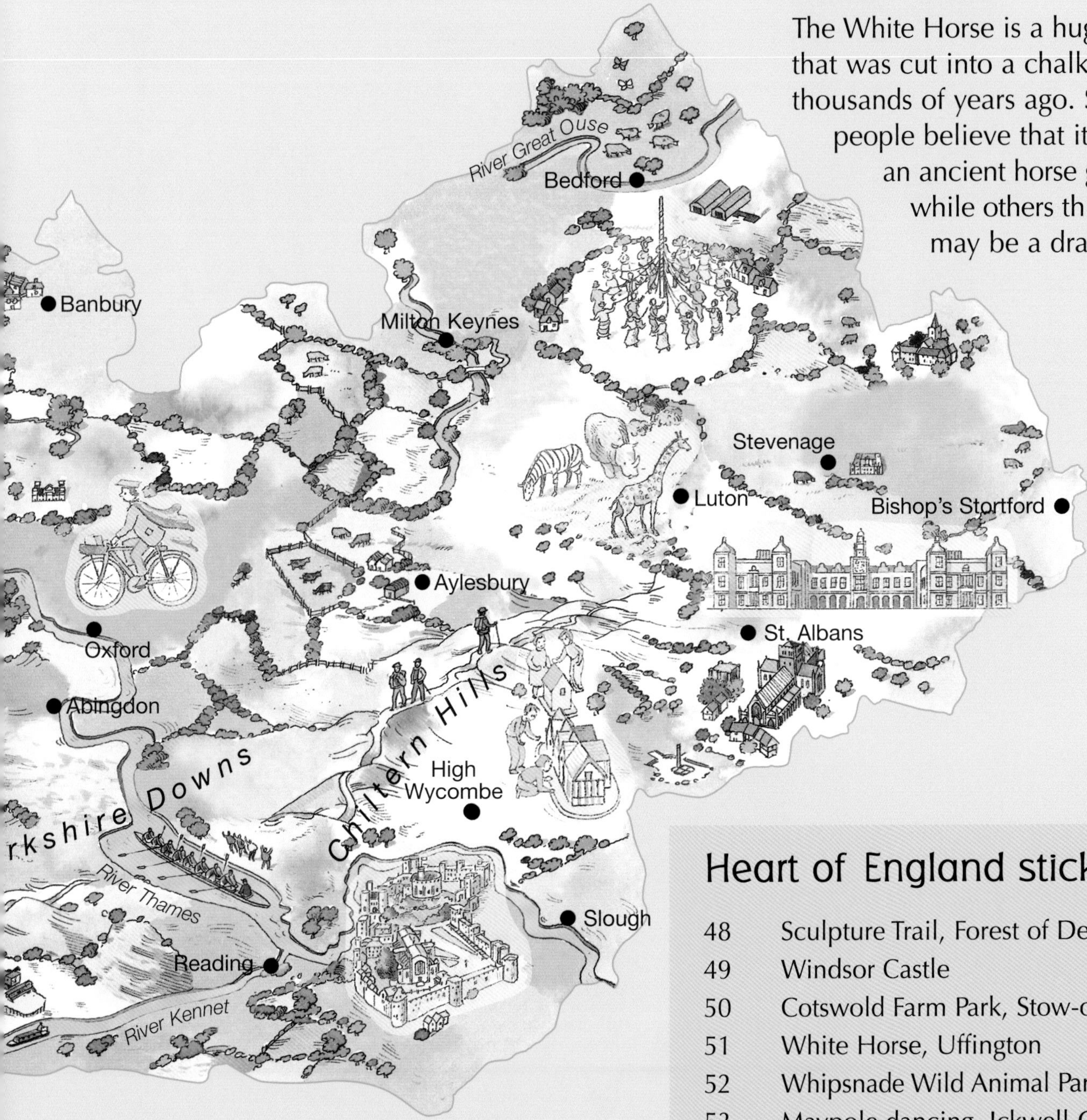

Heart of England stickers

48	Sculpture Trail, Forest of Dean
49	Windsor Castle
50	Cotswold Farm Park, Stow-on-the-Wold
51	White Horse, Uffington
52	Whipsnade Wild Animal Park, Dunstable
53	Maypole dancing, Ickwell Green
54	Student, Oxford University
55	Clifton Suspension Bridge, Bristol
56	Stonehenge
57	Wildfowl and Wetlands Centre, Slimbridge
58	Maze, Longleat House, Warminster
59	Georgian houses, Bath
60	Hatfield House
61	Stone circle, Avebury
62	Bekonscot Model Village, Beaconsfield

Ancient stone circles

More than 5,000 years ago, many rings of stone pillars were constructed in the English countryside. Two of the most spectacular sites are Stonehenge and Avebury, where many of the stones still stand. No one is sure what the circles were for. They may have been ancient temples or burial sites.

East Anglia

East Anglia is the round part of eastern England that juts out into the North Sea. It is famous for its flat landscape, known as the Fens. This area was once marshland, but has now been drained, leaving rich soil, which is ideal for growing grain, fruit and vegetables.

Louth

Lincolnshire Wolds

Skegness

Lincoln

Boston

Grantham

The Wash

King's Lynn

Wisbech

The Fens

Peterborough

River Great Ouse

Ely

East Dereham

Norwich

River Yare

Norfolk Broads

Great Yarmouth

Lowestoft

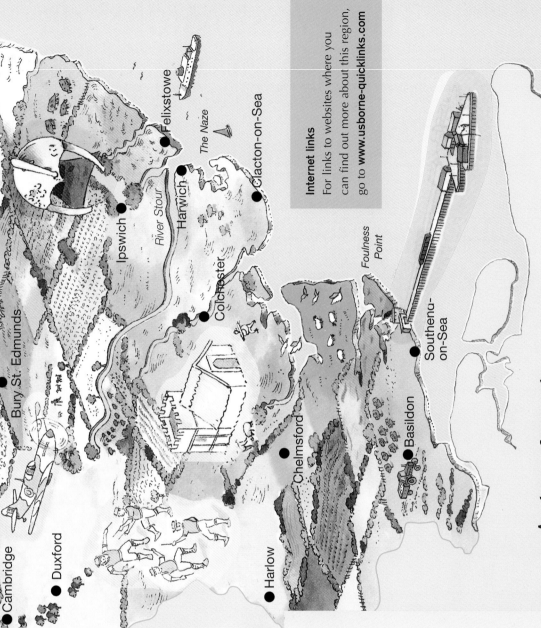

Internet links

For links to websites where you can find out more about this region, go to www.usborne-quicklinks.com

Sunken treasure

Some people believe that treasure belonging to King John of England lies at the bottom of a North Sea inlet called the Wash. In 1216, carts carrying all the king's jewels are said to have got stuck in quicksand near the Wash and then been swept away when the tide came in.

A ship of jewels

In 1939, an archaeologist discovered graves of Anglo-Saxon kings at Sutton Hoo, near Woodbridge. All kinds of treasures had been buried with the kings, including an enormous boat filled with gold, silver and jewels.

East Anglia stickers

63　King John's treasure, the Wash
64　Great Yarmouth Pleasure Beach
65　Morris dancing, Thaxted
66　Cambridge University
67　Traditional thatched house, Norfolk
68　Showjumping, Burghley Park
69　Norman castle reconstruction, Stansted Mountfitchet
70　Lincoln Cathedral
71　Windpump, the Fens
72　Treasure, Mildenhall
73　Imperial War Museum, Duxford
74　Pier, Southend-on-Sea
75　Grimes Graves flint mine, Thetford
76　Sutton Hoo burial site, Woodbridge
77　Sailing, Norfolk Broads

The West Midlands

Internet links
For links to websites where you can find out more about this region, go to **www.usborne-quicklinks.com**

The Midlands make up central England, and the western part extends to the Welsh border. The area has a long history of making pottery, china, chocolate and many other products.

Stafford

Shrewsbury

Cannock   Lichfield   Tamworth

Wolverhampton

Birmingham   Nuneaton

Kidderminster   Coventry   Rugby

Redditch

Worcester   Stratford-upon-Avon

River Wye

River Severn

River Avon

Hereford

Malvern Hills

Shakespeare's home

The playwright William Shakespeare was born in the town of Stratford-upon-Avon in 1564. Thousands of visitors flock there every year to see the house where he was born, and to watch performances of his plays by the Royal Shakespeare Company.

West Midlands stickers

78   Acton Scott Historic Working Farm
79   Iron Bridge, Telford
80   Cadbury World, Bournville
81   Warwick Castle
82   Shakespearean play, Stratford-upon-Avon
83   Pottery factories
84   Book shops, Hay-on-Wye
85   Ludlow Castle

The East Midlands

The East Midlands have lots of scenic countryside, including the Peak District and Sherwood Forest.

Peak District

Buxton

Stoke-on-Trent

River Derwent

Worksop

Mansfield

Sherwood Forest

Newark-on-Trent

Derby

Nottingham

Loughborough

Melton Mowbray

Leicester

Corby

Kettering

Northampton

Robin Hood

Robin Hood was a legendary outlaw and hero who is said to have lived in Sherwood Forest in the Middle Ages. Many stories are told of his daring adventures.

Deer dance

The village of Abbots Bromley has an annual event called the Horn Dance. It dates back to the thirteenth century and involves local men performing dances while carrying deer antlers.

East Midlands stickers

Internet links

For links to websites where you can find out more about this region, go to www.usborne-quicklinks.com

Northwest England

In the far northwest of England is the Lake District, a huge national park that contains beautiful lakes and mountains and is a popular place for walking, sailing and climbing trips. Further south are the busy cities of Liverpool and Manchester.

Beatrix Potter

Beatrix Potter wrote and illustrated famous stories about Peter Rabbit and other characters. She was born in 1866 in London, but she loved the Lake District and spent most of her time there.

Internet links

For links to websites where you can find out more about this region, go to **www.usborne-quicklinks.com**

Carlisle

Penrith

Kendal

Keswick

Scafell Pike

Lake District

SOLWAY FIRTH

Pennines

Workington

Whitehaven

St. Bees Head

Isle of Man

Douglas

133

169

25

37

129

52

141

138

152

24

83

43

175

112

22

32

33

50

45

38

47

59

164

123

53

88

172

72

82

99

71

153

73

104

69

46

65

74

199

78

93

5

109

187

89

63

79

85

75

84

3

41

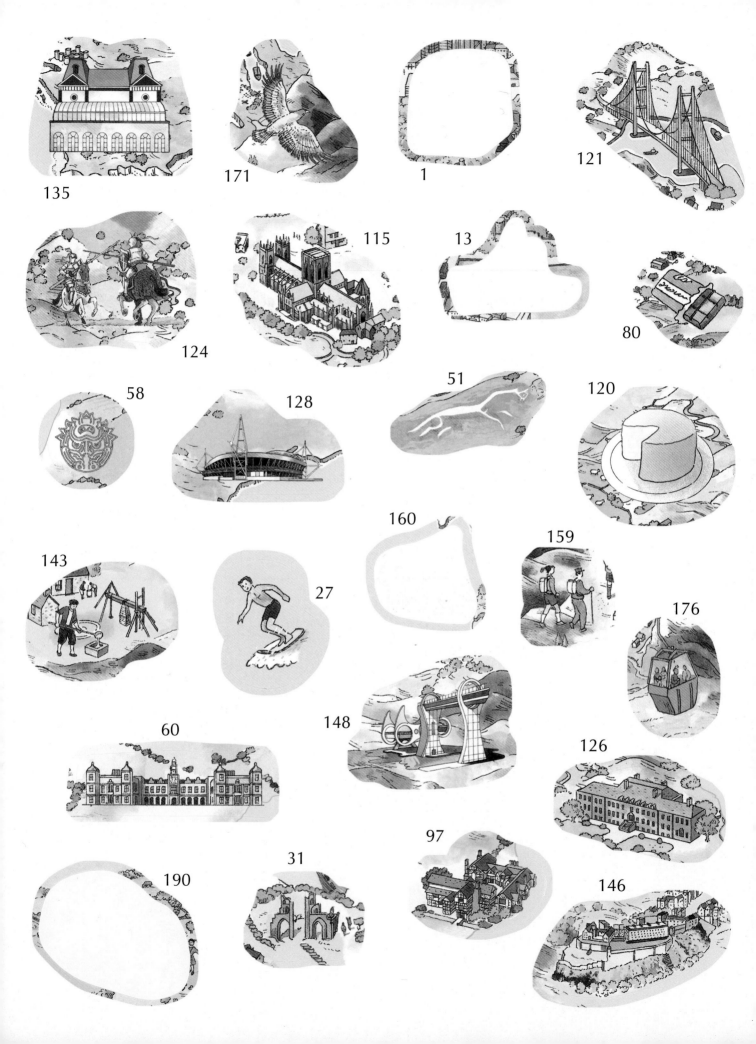

135

171

1

121

124

115

13

80

58

128

51

120

143

27

160

159

176

60

148

126

190

31

97

146

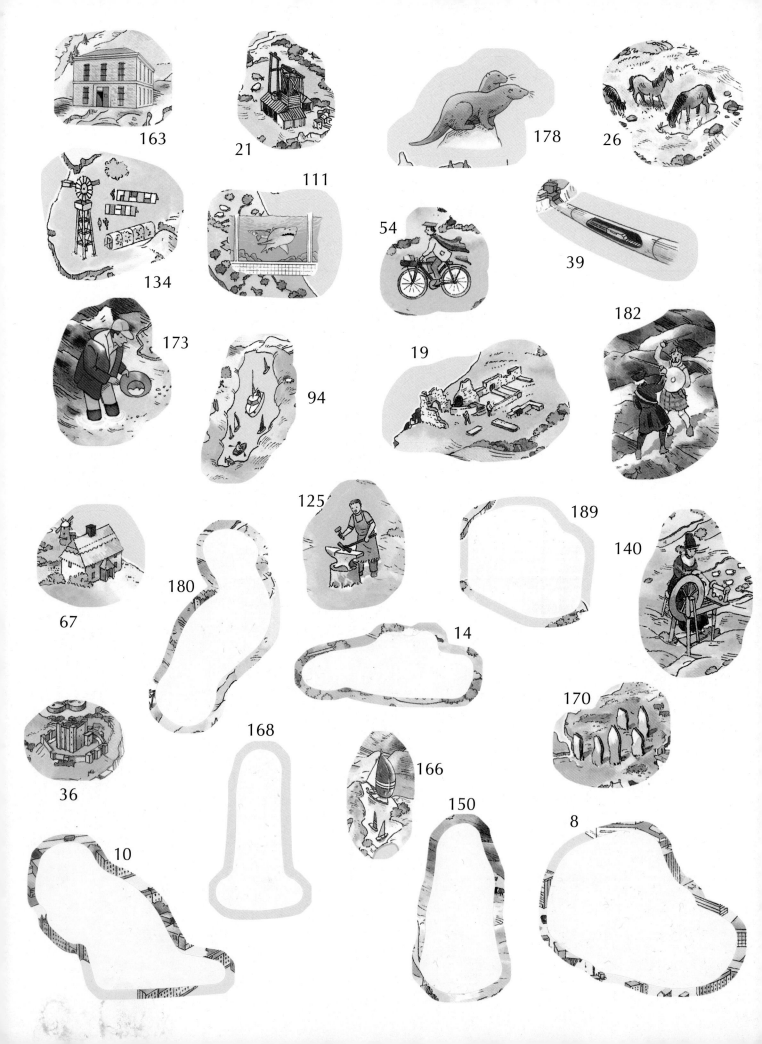

163

21

178

26

111

54

39

134

182

173

19

94

125

189

140

67

180

14

170

36

168

166

150

10

8

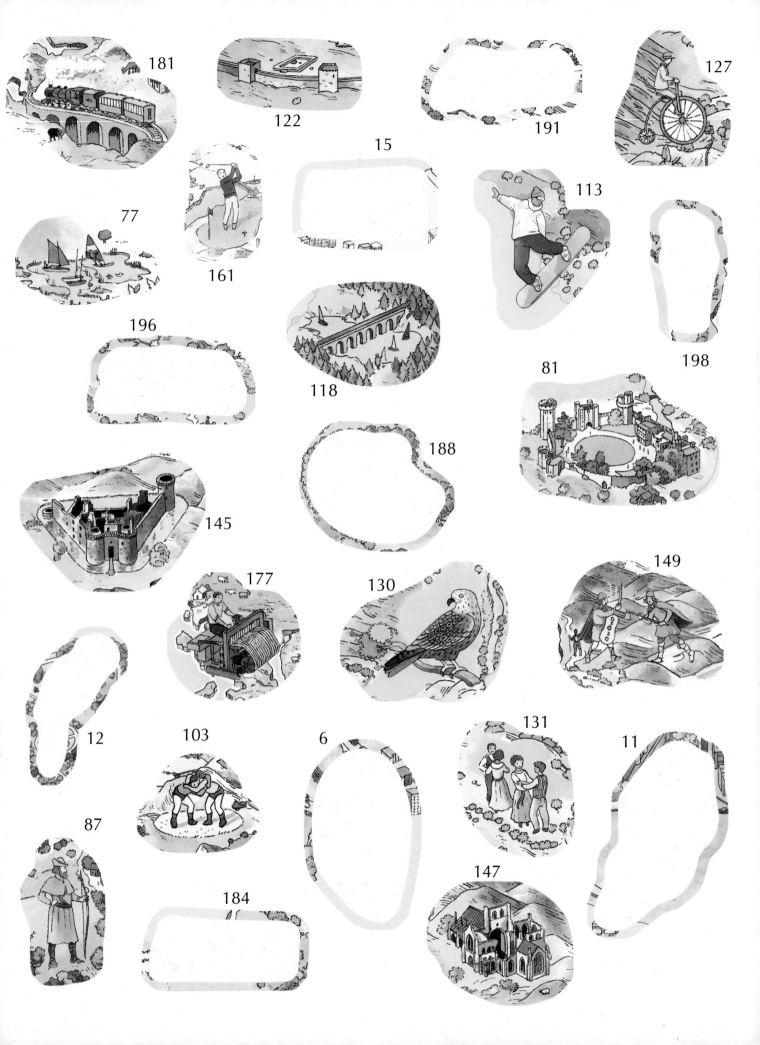

181

122

191

127

15

77

161

113

198

196

118

81

188

145

149

177

130

12

103

6

131

11

87

147

184

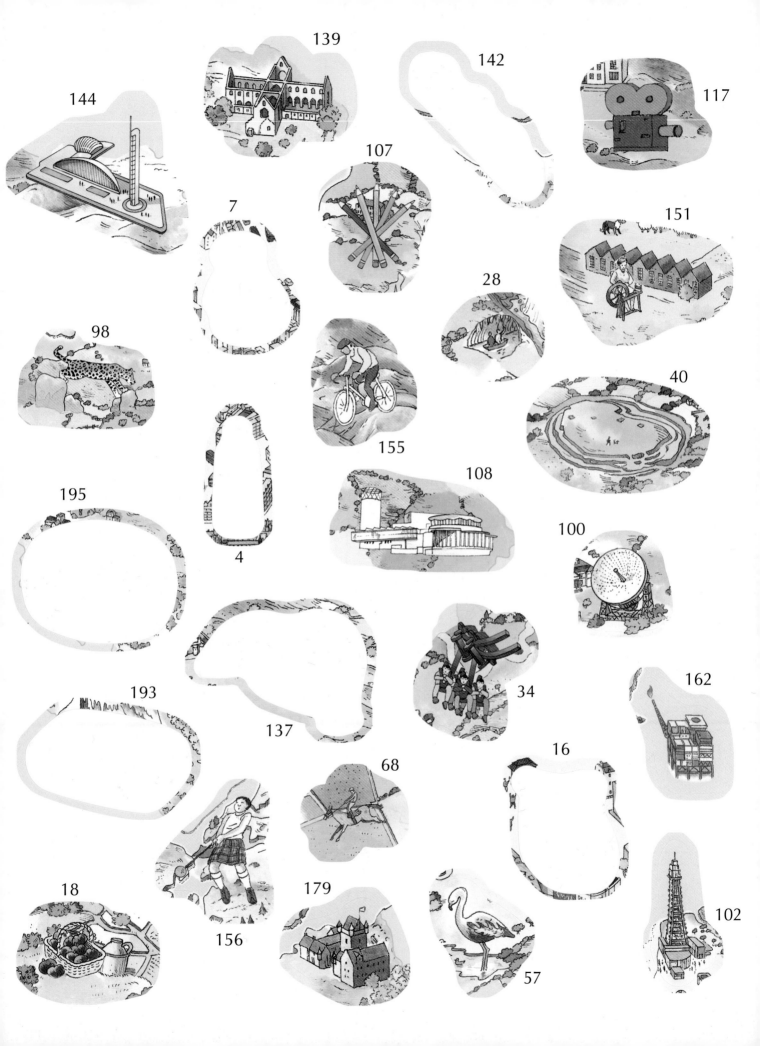

144

139

142

117

107

7

151

28

98

155

40

195

4

108

100

193

137

34

162

68

16

18

156

179

57

102

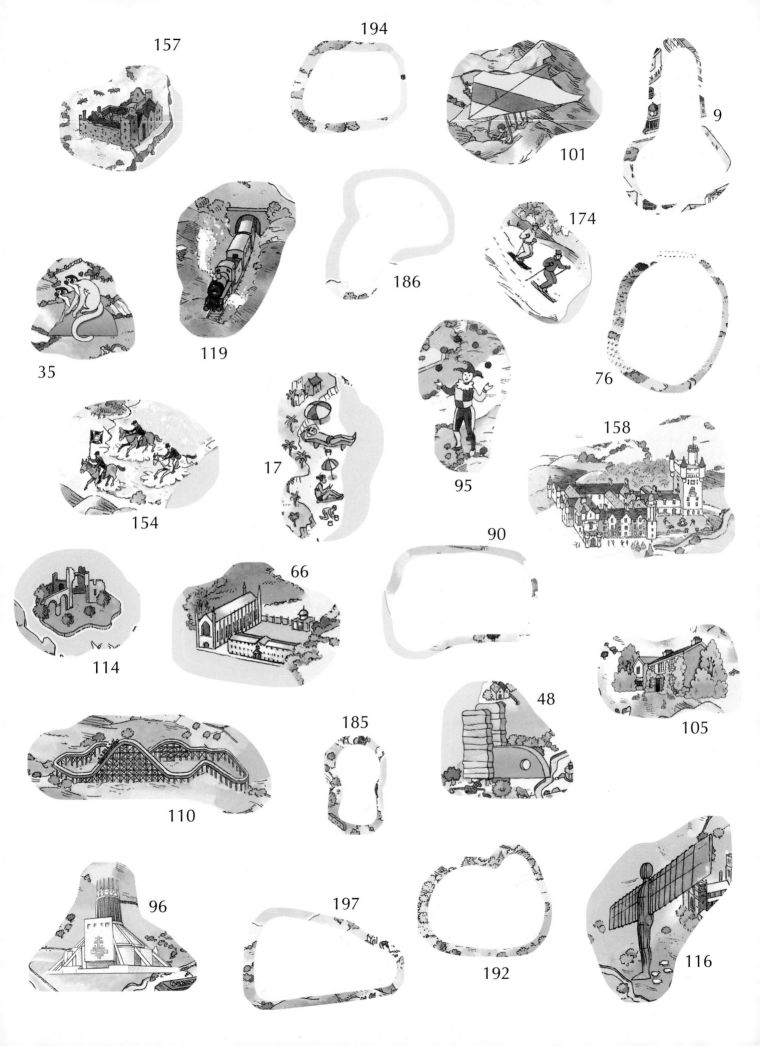

157

194

101

9

119

186

174

35

76

154

17

95

158

114

66

90

105

110

185

48

96

197

192

116

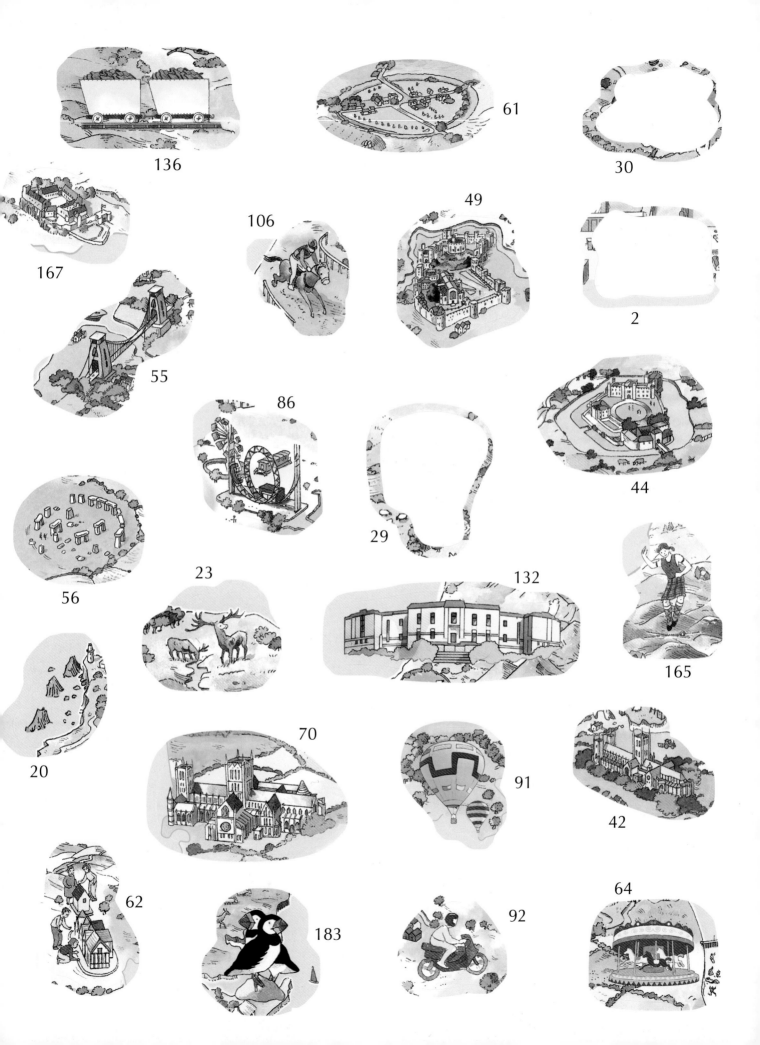

136

61

30

167

106

49

2

55

86

29

44

56

23

132

165

20

70

91

42

62

183

92

64

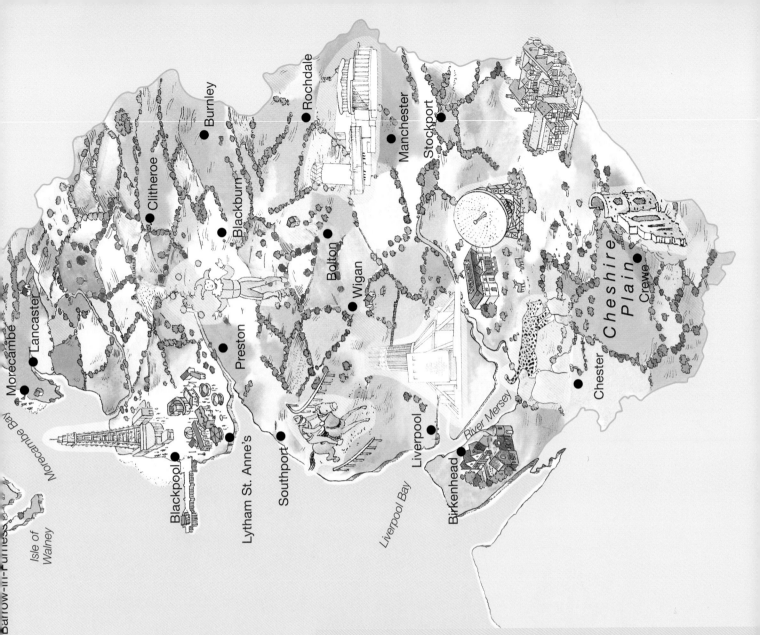

IRISH
SEA

Blackpool

Blackpool is one of Britain's busiest seaside resorts. It has a zoo, three piers, funfair rides and many other kinds of amusements. Its most famous building is Blackpool Tower, which was modelled on the Eiffel Tower, in Paris. It contains a ballroom, an aquarium and a circus.

Northwest England stickers

94   Lake Windermere
95   Camelot theme park, Chorley
96   Liverpool Metropolitan Cathedral
97   Little Moreton Hall, Congleton
98   Chester Zoo
99   Lady Isabella waterwheel
100 Lovell Telescope, Jodrell Bank
101 Hang-gliding, Lake District
102 Blackpool Tower
103 Cumberland and Westmoreland
       wrestling
104 Mow Cop Castle
105 Beatrix Potter's home
106 Horseracing, Aintree racecourse
107 Cumberland Pencil Museum, Keswick
108 The Lowry, Salford

Barrow-in-Furness

Isle of Walney

Morecambe

Morecambe Bay

Lancaster

Clitheroe

Burnley

Blackburn

Preston

Lytham St. Anne's

Blackpool

Southport

Rochdale

Bolton

Wigan

Manchester

Stockport

Liverpool

Liverpool Bay

Birkenhead

River Mersey

Chester

Cheshire Plain

Crewe

Northeast England

Northeast England has huge areas of rugged, windswept countryside. There are also many picturesque cities, including Durham and York.

Northeast England stickers

109 Trams, Beamish Open Air Museum
110 Lightwater Valley theme park
111 The Deep, Kingston upon Hull
112 Medieval fair, Alnwick
113 Ski Village, Sheffield
114 Holy Island (Lindisfarne)
115 York Minster
116 Angel of the North, Gateshead
117 National Museum of Photography, Film and Television, Bradford
118 Kielder Water
119 North Yorkshire Moors Railway
120 Cheese-making, Wensleydale
121 Humber Bridge
122 Hadrian's Wall
123 The Locomotion, Darlington Railway Museum
124 Jousting re-enactment, Royal Armouries Museum, Leeds

Internet links
For links to websites where you can find out more about this region, go to
www.usborne-quicklinks.com

Berwick-upon-Tweed

Cheviot Hills

Ashington

Tynemouth

South Shields

Sunderland

Newcastle-upon-Tyne

Durham

Hartlepool

Redcar

River Wear

River Tees

NORTH SEA

Robin Hood's Bay

Whitby

Scarborough

Flamborough Head

Bridlington Bay

Bridlington

Yorkshire Wolds

Pennines

Skipton

Ripon

Harrogate

York

River Ouse

Kingston upon Hull

Grimsby

Scunthorpe

Leeds

Bradford

Huddersfield

Barnsley

Doncaster

Rotherham

Sheffield

Roman wall

About 2,000 years ago, much of Britain was ruled by the Romans. Emperor Hadrian ordered the building of a wall to mark the northern border of their land and to keep out tribes from further north. Parts of the wall still stand.

Medieval glass

York Minster is a magnificent cathedral that was built in the Middle Ages. It has 128 stained glass windows, and the East Window is the largest piece of medieval stained glass in the world.

Sharks at The Deep

The Deep is a high-tech aquarium where visitors can take an underwater elevator through a gigantic tank and see sharks, rays, eels and other amazing creatures up close.

Wales

Wales is a country of high mountains and deep valleys. Its capital is Cardiff, in the southeast. In the Middle Ages, Wales was often invaded by the English, and many big stone castles were built there.

Welsh festivals

Wales has a yearly folk festival called the Eisteddfod, which means "gathering" in Welsh. It is a week-long celebration of Welsh culture, and is held in a different place each year. There is also a musical Eisteddfod in Llangollen every July, where competitors from around the world take part in music, dance and song contests.

Going underground

Coal mining was once a vital industry in Wales. The Big Pit mine in Blaenafon shut in 1980 and is now a mining museum. Visitors go 90m (300ft) underground to learn what life was like for the many miners who used to dig for coal there.

Liverpool Bay

Flint

Rhyl

Welshpool

Newtown

Radnor Forest

Llandrindod Wells

Great Ormes Head

Llandudno

Bangor

Blaenau Ffestiniog

Dolgellau

Cambrian Mountains

Anglesey

Holy Island

Holyhead

Caernarfon Bay

Porthmadog

Pwllheli

Tremadog Bay

Bardsey Island

Braich y Pwll

Cardigan Bay

Aberystwyth

Aberaeron

Wales stickers

125 Museum of Welsh Life, St. Fagans
126 Erddig Hall, Wrexham
127 National Cycle Exhibition,
     Llandrindod Wells
128 Millennium Stadium, Cardiff
129 Caernarfon Castle
130 Red kite, Cambrian Mountains
131 International Music Eisteddfod, Llangollen
132 National Library of Wales, Aberystwyth
133 Anglesey Sea Zoo
134 Centre for Alternative Technology,
     Machynlleth
135 Grand Theatre, Swansea
136 Big Pit coal mine, Blaenafon
137 King Arthur's Labyrinth, Corris
138 Dinosaur Park, Abercrave
139 Tintern Abbey
140 National Woollen Museum, Llandysul

Southern Scotland

Southern Scotland is known as the Lowlands, because it has fewer mountains than northern Scotland. Scotland's capital city, Edinburgh, is in the south, as is the country's biggest city, Glasgow.

A royal castle

Edinburgh Castle stands on an enormous rock, high above the city. The castle was the home of Scottish kings and is made up of many buildings, including a 12th-century chapel.

Internet links
For links to websites where you can find out more about this region, go to www.usborne-quicklinks.com

St. Abb's Head

North Berwick

Firth of Forth

EDINBURGH

Lammermuir Hills

Pentland Hills

Peebles

Hamilton

River Clyde

Glasgow

Paisley

Kilmarnock

Irvine

River Clyde

Greenock

Firth of Clyde

Southern Scotland stickers

141 Dolphins, Solway Firth
142 Forth Rail Bridge
143 Museum of Lead Mining, Wanlockhead
144 Glasgow Science Centre
145 Caerlaverock Castle
146 Edinburgh Castle
147 Melrose Abbey
148 Falkirk Wheel boat lift
149 Vikingar exhibition, Largs
150 Robert Burns statue, Dumfries
151 Wool mill, Galashiels
152 Fishing, Solway Firth
153 Blowplain Farm, Balmaclellan
154 Common Riding Festival, Selkirk
155 Mountain biking, Southern Uplands

Robert Burns

Scotland's best-known poet is Robert Burns. He was born in Alloway on 25 January 1759, and later lived in Dumfries. His birthday is remembered every year with a celebration called Burns Night.

Cheviot Hills

Southern Uplands

River Teviot

Moffat

Lockerbie

Dumfries

Solway Firth

Castle Douglas

Wigtown Bay

Ayr

Girvan

Stranraer

Luce Bay

Mull of Galloway

Loch Ryan

Moray Firth

Central Scotland

Central Scotland is made up of lowland areas around the east coast. Further west, mountainous land, known as the Highlands, stretches up into northern Scotland.

ATLANTIC
OCEAN

*Grampian
Mountains*

Tobermory

Pitlochry

Coll

Strathmore

Tiree

Mull

Staffa

Ulva

Perth

Iona

Firth of Lorn

Colonsay

Stirling

Jura

Dunfermline

Sound of Jura

Loch Fyne

Dunoon

Whale-watching

Inner Hebrides

Bowmore

Islay

Bute

The sea around the Hebrides Islands is one of the best places in Britain to spot whales. Dolphins, porpoises, seals and even sharks can often be seen there too.

Arran

Campbeltown

Firth of Clyde

Kintyre

Mull of
Kintyre

24

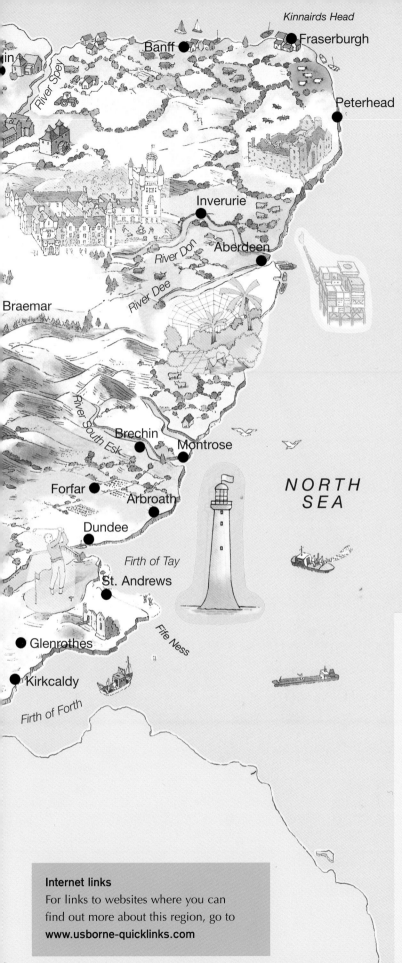

Traditional sports

The Highland Games are displays of traditional Scottish sports, dance and music, and are held in towns throughout Scotland every summer. Events such as throwing heavy weights or tossing the caber, a huge, trimmed tree trunk, require a lot of strength.

Creepy castle

Slains Castle stands on a jagged cliff edge on the North Sea coast. It was built in 1597 and is now in ruins. The author Bram Stoker visited the castle in 1895, and might have used it in his novel *Dracula* as the model for Dracula's spooky home.

Central Scotland stickers

Internet links
For links to websites where you can find out more about this region, go to **www.usborne-quicklinks.com**

Northern Scotland

Northern Scotland is one of the most unspoilt parts of Britain. Its stunning Highland scenery includes mountains, moors and lochs, which are lakes or long sea inlets.

ATLANTIC OCEAN

Cape Wrath

Butt of Lewis

Eddrachillis Bay

Stornoway

Lewis

Outer Hebrides

Harris

The Minch

Gruinard Bay

Ullapool

Loch Torridon

North Uist

Benbecula

Inner Hebrides

South Uist

Portree

Skye

Cuillin Hills

Kyle of Lochalsh

Barra

Loch monster

There are many stories about a giant, humpbacked monster that is said to live in Loch Ness. Some people claim to have caught glimpses of a strange creature there, but nothing has ever been proved.

Rhum (Rum)

Eigg

Mallaig

Sound of Sleat

Point of Ardnamurchan

Glen M

Ben Nevis

Fort William

Loch Linnhe

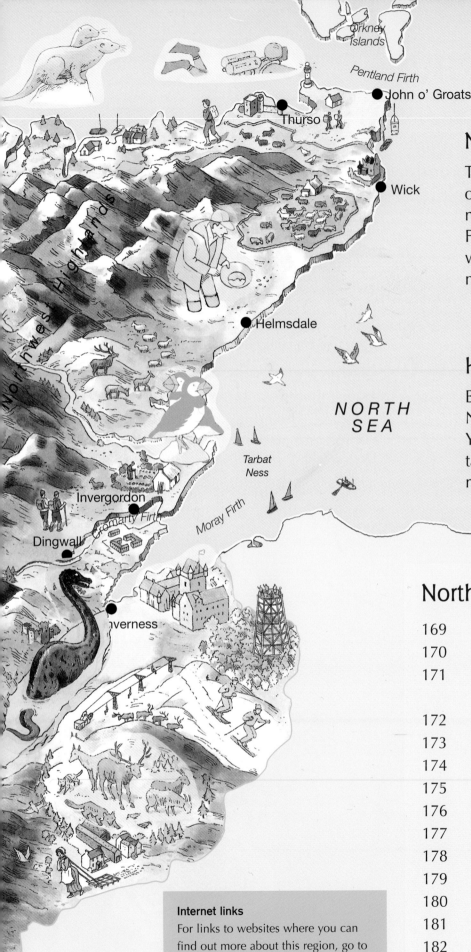

Orkney
Islands

To the Shetland
Islands ↗

Pentland Firth

John o' Groats

Thurso

Wick

Helmsdale

NORTH
SEA

Tarbat
Ness

Invergordon

Cromarty Firth

Moray Firth

Dingwall

Inverness

Northern islands

The Orkney Islands are a group
of scenic islands just off the
northeast tip of mainland Scotland.
Further north still are the rugged,
windswept Shetland Islands, the
most northerly part of Britain.

High ride

Britain's highest mountain, Ben
Nevis, is 1,343m (4,406ft) high.
You can get good views of it by
taking a cable car up a nearby
mountain called Aonach Mor.

Northern Scotland stickers

169	Highland Wildlife Park, Kincraig
170	Calanais Standing Stones, Lewis
171	Golden eagle, Beinn Eighe nature reserve
172	Diving for wrecks, Pentland Firth
173	Panning for gold, Baile an Or
174	Ski resort, Aviemore
175	Skye Serpentarium, Broadford
176	Cable car, Aonach Mor
177	Harris tweed worker
178	Sea otters, Kyle of Tongue
179	Cawdor Castle
180	Loch Ness monster
181	Glenfinnan Viaduct
182	Historical weapons show, Clansman Centre, Fort Augustus
183	Puffins, Dornoch Firth

Internet links
For links to websites where you can
find out more about this region, go to
www.usborne-quicklinks.com

Northern Ireland

 Northern Ireland's varied landscape includes mountains, farmland and lakes called loughs. Its capital is Belfast, a large city which is home to around a sixth of the country's population.

Ireland's saint

On March 17th, Irish people celebrate St. Patrick's Day. St. Patrick was a famous fifth-century bishop who is buried in Downpatrick.

Belfast cranes

Samson and Goliath are two towering cranes that belong to a shipbuilding company. They dominate the Belfast skyline and are well-known symbols of Belfast's long history of shipbuilding.

Northern Ireland stickers

184	Samson and Goliath cranes, Belfast
185	Tenth century stone cross, Ardboe
186	Giant's Causeway
187	Devenish Monastery
188	Peatlands Country Park, Dungannon
189	Ulster Folk and Transport Museum
190	St. Patrick's Day parade, Downpatrick
191	Dunluce Castle
192	Ulster History Park
193	Marble Arch Caves
194	Spanish Armada treasure, Ulster Museum, Belfast
195	Navan Fort, Armagh
196	Hurling game, Maghera
197	Medieval city walls, Londonderry
198	Dodo Terrace, Mount Stewart House, Newtownards
199	Ulster American Folk Park, Omagh

Londonderry (Derry)

River F

Straba

Oma

Lower Lough Erne

Enniskillen

Upper Lough Erne

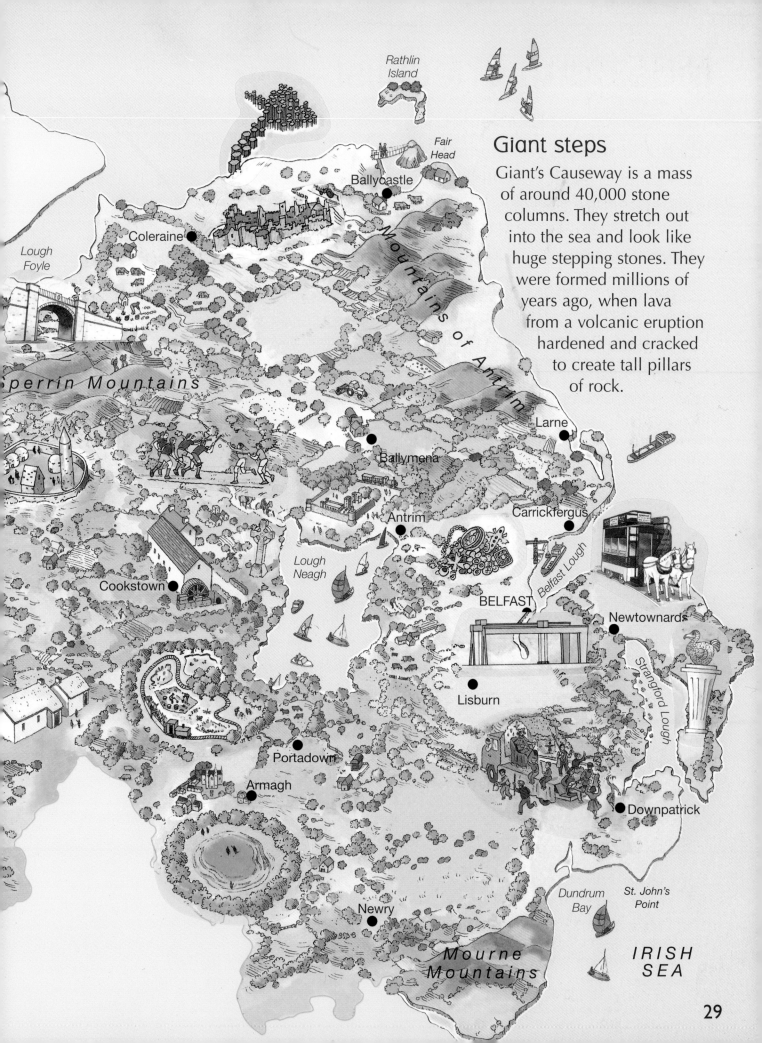

Giant steps

Giant's Causeway is a mass of around 40,000 stone columns. They stretch out into the sea and look like huge stepping stones. They were formed millions of years ago, when lava from a volcanic eruption hardened and cracked to create tall pillars of rock.

Rathlin Island

Fair Head

Ballycastle

Coleraine

Lough Foyle

Sperrin Mountains

Mountains of Antrim

Larne

Ballymena

Carrickfergus

Antrim

Lough Neagh

Belfast Lough

Cookstown

BELFAST

Newtownards

Lisburn

Strangford Lough

Portadown

Armagh

Downpatrick

Newry

Dundrum Bay

St. John's Point

Mourne Mountains

IRISH SEA

Index and checklist

This checklist will help you to find where the stickers go. The first number after each entry tells you which page the sticker is on. The second number is the number next to the sticker.

Edited by Gillian Doherty and Louie Stowell
Cartographic editor: Craig Asquith
Consultants: Dr. Gillian McIntosh, Queen's University Belfast;
Dr. James Oliver, University of Edinburgh;
Dr. Paul Readman, King's College London;
Dr. Steven Thompson, University of Wales, Aberystwyth
With thanks to Fiona Patchett and Alice Pearcey
Cover design by Stephen Moncrieff and Sam Chandler
Digital manipulation by Katie Mayes, Mike Olley
and Nick Wakeford